If you are going to do the wrong thing,
you better be right.
— Caio

Eat less, move more.

Lightning Source UK Ltd.
Milton Keynes UK
UKOW01n1513241017
311578UK00003B/271/P

9 781389 565373